The rapid growth of academic literature in the field of economics has posed serious problems for both students and teachers of the subject. The latter find it difficult to keep pace with more than a few areas of their subject, so that an inevitable trend towards specialism emerges. The student quickly loses perspective as the maze of theories and models grows and the discipline accommodates an increasing amount of quantitative techniques.

'Macmillan Studies in Economics' is a new series which sets out to provide the student with short, reasonably critical surveys of the developments within the various specialist areas of theoretical and applied economics. At the same time, the studies aim to form an integrated series so that, seen as a whole, they supply a balanced overview of the subject of economics. The emphasis in each study is upon recent work, but each topic will generally be placed in a historical context so that the reader may see the logical development of thought through time. Selected bibliographies are provided to guide readers to more extensive works. Each study aims at a brief treatment of the salient problems in order to avoid clouding the issues in detailed argument. Nonetheless, the texts are largely self-contained, and presume only that the student has some knowledge of elementary micro-economics and macro-economics.

Mathematical exposition has been adopted only where necessary. Some recent developments in economics are not readily comprehensible without some mathematics and statistics, and quantitative approaches also serve to shorten what would otherwise be lengthy and involved arguments. Where authors have found it necessary to introduce mathematical techniques, these techniques have been kept to a minimum. The emphasis is upon the economics, and not upon the quantitative methods. Later studies in the series will provide analyses of the links between quantitative methods, in particular econometrics, and economic analysis.

MACMILLAN STUDIES IN ECONOMICS

General Editors: D. C. ROWAN and G. R. FISHER
Executive Editor: D. W. PEARCE

Published
John Burton: WAGE INFLATION
Miles Fleming: MONETARY THEORY
C. J. Hawkins and D. W. Pearce: CAPITAL INVESTMENT APPRAISAL
David F. Heathfield: PRODUCTION FUNCTIONS
D. W. Pearce: COST-BENEFIT ANALYSIS
R. Shone: THE PURE THEORY OF INTERNATIONAL TRADE
Grahame Walshe: INTERNATIONAL MONETARY REFORM

Forthcoming
E. R. Chang: PRINCIPLES OF ECONOMIC ACCOUNTING
G. Denton: ECONOMICS OF INDICATIVE PLANNING
N. Gibson: MONETARY POLICY
C. J. Hawkins: THEORY OF THE FIRM
D. Jackson: THE ECONOMICS OF POVERTY
P. N. Junankar: INVESTMENT FUNCTIONS
J. E. King: LABOUR ECONOMICS
J. Kregel: THEORY OF ECONOMIC GROWTH
D. Mayston: THE POSSIBILITY OF SOCIAL CHOICE
G. McKenzie: MONETARY THEORY OF INTERNATIONAL TRADE
S. K. Nath: WELFARE ECONOMICS
F. Pennance: HOUSING ECONOMICS
Maurice Peston: PUBLIC GOODS AND THE PUBLIC SECTOR
David Robertson: INTERNATIONAL TRADE POLICY
C. Rowley: ANTI-TRUST ECONOMICS
C. Sharp: TRANSPORT ECONOMICS
G. K. Shaw: FISCAL POLICY
P. Simmons: DEMAND THEORY
M. Stabler: AGRICULTURAL ECONOMICS
Frank J. B. Stilwell: REGIONAL ECONOMIC POLICY
M. Townsend: QUANTITY THEORY OF MONEY
M. Townsend: MONETARISM VERSUS KEYNESIANISM
John Vaizey: ECONOMICS OF EDUCATION
P. Victor: ECONOMICS OF POLLUTION

Monetary Theory

MILES FLEMING

Professor of Economics, University of Bristol

Macmillan

First published 1972 by
THE MACMILLAN PRESS LTD
London and Basingstoke
Associated companies in New York Toronto
Dublin Melbourne Johannesburg and Madras

SBN 333 11842 1

Printed in Great Britain by
THE ANCHOR PRESS LTD
Tiptree, Essex

Contents

Acknowledgements

I wish to thank Professor D. C. Rowan and Dr. J. A. Kregel for their valuable suggestions on my manuscript.

M.F.

1 Introduction

This short monograph attempts a critical synthesis of modern contributions to monetary theory. It aims to give a coherent picture of the whole field by stressing the interrelations between its various elements. While it is not a summary of contending views, it does give numerous references to the literature in which such views can be studied in detail; extensive reviews of that literature are available elsewhere [23, 25]. Within the space available it is possible to consider only major aspects of the subject and to assess the state of current theory in relation to them. Selection and judgement in these respects are those of the author.

The concern here is with monetary *theory*, i.e. with the construction and analysis of hypotheses about the interaction of money and economic activity. But theory has to be tested. One of the distinctive features of monetary economics in the last decade or so has been the growth of econometric work. That is not discussed here.

2 The Definition of Money

There is a long history of disagreements on the definition of money ([15] chaps. 2, 3; [36]). Two aspects of the problem must be distinguished. First, precisely what qualities must a thing have in order to be called money? This question about the *concept* of money has centred on the qualities of being a means of payment, a store of value and a unit of account. Second, what in fact are the particular things at any time to which the concept of money refers? This question concerns the empirical *content* of the concept of money. It is a particularly pressing problem when the quantity of money has to be measured for econometric work.

Agreement on the concept of money is needed for communication between people. But more fundamentally, the agreement should have a purpose. In a scientific subject, the agreed definition of money must be 'useful' : it must be usable in the framing of theories which explain the working of the economic system. The test of the 'goodness' of a definition of money can therefore be only an indirect one. The definition will be good in so far as it is an element in a valid economic theory.

Some of the difficulties in defining money can be seen by considering the notion of a means of payment. Coin, bank notes and demand deposits at commercial banks are means of payment since they are generally acceptable in exchange for goods and financial assets (e.g. bonds and shares). Time deposits at commercial banks cannot be transferred by cheque and would therefore appear not to be a means of payment. Yet banks will usually honour cheques drawn against insufficient demand deposits if their clients have adequate time deposits.

But goods and financial assets can also be acquired on credit. For example, transactions between firms involve 'trade credit', and dealings on some stock exchanges are carried out 'on account'.

These credits have of course to be settled in time with a generally acceptable means of payment (though some may be cleared by offsetting book entries). It may therefore be said that credit is not a means of payment. Nevertheless the two are, to some extent, substitute ways of acquiring goods and financial assets.

Suppose we say that the means of payment function is a necessary part of the concept of money. This leads to some difficulties about the empirical content of the concept, e.g. whether time deposits, as well as demand deposits, should be included. But, however the problem of content is settled, it still leaves open the question of the *degree of substitutability* between money and credit as alternative ways of acquiring goods and financial assets. This is clearly an important matter because of its possible effect on the relationship between the level of spending and the quantity of money.

A means of payment, by its very nature, must also be a store of value. It must be capable of being held, however briefly, in the time interval between its receipt from a sale and its use in an ensuing purchase. A means of payment is necessarily an asset and is therefore one form in which personal wealth can be held through time. This brings out the main reason why the concept of money has been so much debated. Money is not a simple concept with only one defining characteristic. It is *both* a means of payment and a store of value. In the latter respect it is therefore a substitute for the other assests in which personal wealth can be held.

At any moment of time, an individual wealth-owner has to choose how to distribute his wealth between real assets (durable goods), financial assets (e.g. bonds and shares) and money. He may of course also have financial liabilities, e.g. he may himself have issued bonds. These enable him to acquire a larger quantity of assets. There are various considerations that will influence his decision as to the amount of money to hold in relation both to his other assets and to any liabilities he may have. These considerations determine the *degree of substitutability* between money on the one hand and real and financial assets on the other.

Particular assets may be more or less 'close', or more or less 'distant', substitutes for money. Indeed the matter is further complicated because the things which act as money may themselves be close, rather than perfect, substitutes for one another. Bank notes are not perfectly substitutable for coins in purchases from vending machines which take only coins; nor are bank deposits perfectly substitutable for notes and coins in shops which will not accept cheques.

There is a spectrum of degrees of substitutability between money and all other assets. One may search for criteria that indicate a 'marked gap' in this spectrum as a means of differentiating money on one side of it from non-monetary assets on the other. The search for such a gap involves an analysis of the *reasons* for people's preferences between different assets, and of the *ways* in which they can and do exercise these preferences. This analysis is a central part of monetary theory. Hence a definition of money, which distinguishes it clearly from other assets, can be arrived at only in the process of constructing, and testing, monetary theories.

However, the construction of a theory must have a starting point, even if it is a provisional one. It will be assumed here that money comprises all those assets that are generally accepted means of payment. The variables which determine the quantity demanded of money in this sense will be investigated in Section 3 below. The corresponding enquiry into the quantity supplied of money will be carried out in Section 4. The ways in which a lack of equality between the quantities demanded and supplied of money may disturb the economy will be analysed in Section 5. And the effects of these disturbances on national output and the price level will be pursued in Section 6.

3 The Demand for Money

It is possible to identify the influences that *could* affect the quantity demanded of money by starting with the analysis of simple situations and working on to more complex ones. Suppose that each household (or firm) is quite certain of both the amounts and the dates of its future receipts and payments of all kinds. It could then plan the minimum money balances to be held from moment to moment that would just be sufficient to enable it to make the expected payments. These balances would be held in the intervals of time between receipts and payments, and their sizes would depend on both the amounts of the receipts and the payments and the lack of synchronisation between them [8]. The latter can be explained in part by conventions as to the time intervals at which certain kinds of payments have to be made (e.g. weekly wage-payments). But it depends as well on the voluntary decisions of households and firms as to the frequencies with which they will purchase goods either for immediate use or to add to stock [6]; and also upon the terms on which credit is granted on purchases.

The quantity demanded of money, in aggregate for the economy, would then depend on the sizes of all the payments on factor incomes, on final expenditures for consumption and investment, on intermediate transactions, on second-hand goods and on financial assets. But if these various categories of expenditure were always to change in the same proportion, the demand for money would vary in direct proportion to the level of national income.

However, individuals need not hold money in the time intervals between receipts and payments. Upon its receipt, they could exchange the money for other assets with the intention of selling these for money just before the next payments are due. If they hold bonds, rather than money, they will gain interest plus or minus any change in the market price of the bond over the period in question (this assumes, as is usually the case, that money does not earn interest). On the other hand, they will incur *transactions costs* in buying and selling the bonds, both in the non-pecuniary form of time and effort spent on the transactions and maybe in the pecuniary form of 'brokerage charges' to middlemen (e.g. stockbrokers) who carry out the transactions for them. Hence the choice between holding money or bonds depends on the balance between the interest, plus capital gains or minus capital losses, to be earned and the transactions costs to be incurred. If the former is firmly expected to outweigh the latter, individuals will reduce the money balances they hold through time by recurrent purchases and sales of bonds in the time intervals between other receipts and payments.

The amount of interest that can be earned on bonds will increase with the length of the intended 'holding period', i.e. the length of time over which it is intended to hold them. But transactions costs are unlikely to vary significantly in this respect. Hence, the longer the time interval between a receipt and its intended disposal, the greater will be the incentive to hold bonds rather than money in the meantime. It will probably not be worthwhile making a short-term loan from part of a salary which is going to be spent entirely on consumption during the coming month; but it will be otherwise with any saving out of the salary that is intended for use in retirement.

Moreover, transactions costs will vary in *smaller* proportion than the value of the bonds purchased. They will not be anything like 1000 times greater on the purchase of bonds worth £1 million than on a purchase worth £1000. Hence business firms with large receipts and payments will find it much more worthwhile to economise on their holding of money, by means of recurrent short-term lending, than will households with small incomes and expenditures.

The analysis so far indicates that the quantity demanded of money will decrease as interest rates rise (given the level of expenditure in the economy). With interest rates higher relative to transactions costs, additional recurrent lending to economise on money balances becomes worthwhile. In this respect, the desired holdings of money can be explained in the same way as the desired holdings of inventories of goods by business firms [1, 42].

Indeed, this suggests the next point. Will individuals consider the holding of durable goods, as well as of bonds (and shares), as being competitive with the holding of money in the time intervals between receipts and payments? Where the amounts and dating of the latter are certain, this seems to be an unimportant possibility, at least for short time intervals. Goods can yield rates of return (e.g. profits on producers' capital) to set against the transactions costs of buying and selling them. But specialised knowledge is usually required to reap these returns; the spread between the buying and the selling prices of durable goods is often considerable; and the transactions costs involved are usually large. On these grounds, the degree of substitutability between money and real assets will be small. But there are further aspects to this matter which will be considered later.

The future receipts and payments, on which the demand for money depends, cannot be predicted with certainty. There are chances that they will be either above or below what are judged to be their most probable values. An individual who is averse to bearing risks will be more concerned with the chances that receipts may be below rather than above their most probable values, and with the opposite chances in the case of payments. Given interest rates and transactions costs, a 'risk-averter' will therefore hold *larger* money balances than would be necessary on the basis of his predictions of the most probable values of future receipts and payment. In that way he 'hedges' against the risks of having to acquire additional money balances; he exercises what Keynes calls a 'precautionary motive' ([27] chap. 15).

But expectations, and their uncertainties, will influence the demand for money in another respect. Financial assets may have fixed prices (e.g. deposits in a non-bank financial intermediary like a building society), or they may have variable prices (as with many government securities). In the case of bonds, their prices will vary inversely with market interest rates. This consideration affects the choice between holding money or bonds in two ways.

First, a firm expectation that interest rates are going to fall (i.e. that bond prices are going to rise) will strengthen the case

15

for holding bonds rather than money. 'Bullish' sentiments will decrease the demand for money. On the other hand, a firmly-expected fall in bond prices (rise in interest rates) could offset, more or less, the interest to be earned on bonds. Hence 'bearish' sentiments will increase the demand for money. It is these interest-rate expectations that underlie Keynes' 'speculative motive' for holding money ([27] chap. 15).

But secondly, interest-rate expectations will not be held with certainty. This provides an additional influence on the choice between bonds and money. Risk-averters will wish to hedge, to some extent, against the chances that future interest rates will be higher (bond prices lower) than their most probable expected levels. This will lead them to hold larger money balances than in the absence of uncertainty about future interest rates. There is thus a precautionary motive arising out of *uncertain* interest-rate expectations which is analogous to that (discussed above) coming from the uncertain amounts and dating of future receipts and payments. This precautionary motive must not be confused with the speculative motive [43].

EXPECTATIONS

Clearly, the relevance of expectations of all kinds to the demand for money needs careful specification. The choice between holding money or other assets (real or financial) depends on the balance between transactions costs and the *uncertain expected* rates of return on assets (which take into account expected changes in their prices). The relative magnitudes of these two sets of influences depends on the length of the intended holding period for money or other assets. The longer that is, the smaller will be the relative importance of transactions costs. On the other hand, the expected returns (and their uncertainties) for different kinds of assets will vary with the length of the holding period. For example, financial assets may have fixed or variable prices; and they have a variety of 'terms to maturity' (as given by the dates at which their issuers are obliged to redeem them). The fixed-price deposits in non-bank financial intermediaries are encashable after a short period of

16

notice; the term to maturity of Treasury bills usually runs up to three months; bonds have lives covering the whole spectrum from very short to very long (and there may be some which, like shares, have no definite redemption dates); and real assets may wear out, or become obsolete, after shorter or longer periods of time.

When individuals hold wealth through time they may expect to consume different portions of it at different, more or less definite, dates in the future. The allocation of wealth between different kinds of assets will depend in part on those expected dates for the consumption of wealth, i.e. on the intended holding periods for the different portions of wealth. Money is a substitute for other assets in respect of all lengths of holding period. But the degrees of substitutability between them will vary with the length of the holding period *because* the relative magnitudes of transactions costs, expected rates of return on assets, and their uncertainties, all vary with the length of the holding period. The nub of the problems concerning the demand for money is to discover the regularities in the determination of those degrees of substitutability.

It has been seen how the expected changes in the prices of financial and real assets must be taken into account in predicting the expected rates of return on them which are relevant to the choice between holding money or other assets. It is now necessary to go further and allow for the expected changes in the *money* prices of the goods that may be acquired in the future out of holdings of money and other assets. Two points in this respect need to be distinguished.

The magnitudes of the future receipts and payments, upon which the demand for money depends in part, are the products of the expected *volumes* and the expected *prices* of the transactions in question. The higher these prices are expected to be, the larger will be the *nominal* amounts of money which individuals will have to hold. The nominal amount of money is that measured in terms of a unit of account (e.g. the pound sterling). It must be distinguished from the *real* amount of money which is measured in terms of the volume of goods that money can purchase. The real value of a given nominal amount of money decreases as prices rise, and vice versa. The first point to be made is

17

that an expected change in the prices of goods will, *in itself,* alter the nominal demand for money in the same proportion; and it will therefore leave the real demand for money unchanged.

The second point is that an expected change in goods prices will probably alter the relative magnitudes of the influences which determine the choice between holding money or other assets. Thus if goods prices are expected to rise, the real value of a nominal unit of money is expected to fall; and so is the real value of a fixed-price financial asset. The real values of variable-price bonds will also be expected to fall unless their money prices are expected to rise (i.e. interest rates to fall) – which is unlikely in the circumstances. If the money prices of all goods are expected to rise in line with one another, the real values of durable goods will not be affected. And if profits are expected to increase along with prices, the real values of shares may not fall.

Thus an expected rise in goods prices will alter *relatively* the expected rates of return on different non-monetary assets; and it will also make some of these assets (e.g. shares and durable goods) relatively more attractive to hold than money. What this means is that the *proportion* of their wealth which individuals want to hold in the form of money (and bonds) will probably be reduced by an expectation of a rise in goods prices. The real demand for money will decrease [9]. But the amount of the decrease will depend also on the additional transactions costs that individuals will incur as they try to economise further on their holdings of (real) money balances. The more steeply transactions costs (in real terms) rise in relation to the volume of transactions, the less will be the substitution of other assets for money as the result of an expected rise in goods prices.

It is necessary, in this respect, to recall that the substitutability between money and other assets varies with the length of the holding period for wealth. Hence the effect on the demand for money of expected rises in prices will depend on for how long, and at what rates, they are expected to continue. It is the expected rates of rise with respect to each holding period, relative to the corresponding transactions costs, that will determine the overall effect on the demand for money. Moreover, there will be uncertainties attaching to these expected price rises which will enter into the uncertainties surrounding the rates of return on different assets. There are 'precautionary' as well as 'speculative' aspects to expected changes in the prices of goods.

The demand for money depends on the proportions of their total assets which households and firms want to hold in a monetary rather than in a non-monetary form. It is possible to hold more assets by incurring more liabilities; this is what a firm does when it borrows or issues shares to finance the acquisition of real assets. It is therefore necessary to distinguish the *gross* total of assets from the *net* total which equals assets minus liabilities. The gross total provides the constraint upon the choice between money and other assets. It is within this total that individuals have to weigh up the rival attractions of different assets. But their demand for money will also depend on the nature and size of their liabilities, because of the prospective payments that may have to be made in settlement of them. (The problems of aggregation in macro-economics are discussed in [29] chap. 3.)

In considering the relations between wealth and the demand for money it is necessary to distinguish between (*a*) what would be the desired holding of money at any desired total of wealth, and (*b*) what would be the desired holding of money when households and firms wish to *change* the totals of their wealth. The former case is concerned with comparisons between (static) equilibrium holdings of assets. The latter deals with (dynamic) changes in the holding of assets. This distinction will enter into the analysis at a later stage.

THE DEMAND FUNCTION

The analysis so far has been directed to identifying the things that could influence the quantity demanded of money. These are the variables which enter into the argument of the demand for money function. It will be necessary, in due course, to ask both how these variables are themselves determined and what are likely to be the magnitudes of the effects which changes in them could have on the quantity demanded of money. It will be helpful therefore to list them precisely with brief commentaries on some of their significant aspects.

19

The *nominal* quantity demanded of money depends on:

(i) The expected dates of future receipts and payments (in nominal terms). It is the lack of synchronisation between these that leads to the holding of some money in the time intervals between them.

(ii) The expected levels of future expenditures. These comprise all payments on both current and capital accounts, and it is *expectations* with respect to them that help to determine the demand for money.

(iii) The degrees of uncertainty attaching to both the amounts and the dates of future receipts and payments. Risk aversion in these respects increases the demand for money.

(iv) The expected levels of prices in the future. The nominal quantity demanded of money depends on the prices of goods on which it may be spent.

(v) The transactions costs involved in switching between money and non-monetary assets.

(vi) The expected rates of return on non-monetary assets (which take into account the most probable expected changes in their prices). These have to be compared, for each intended holding period for wealth, with the corresponding transactions costs to discover whether it is worthwhile to hold a non-monetary asset rather than money during the period in question.

(vii) The degrees of uncertainty attaching to the expected rates of return on non-monetary assets. Risk aversion in these respects increases the demand for money.

(viii) The expected rates of change (and their uncertainties) in the prices of goods in the future. These will affect the expected rates of return (and their uncertainties) on non-monetary assets both relative to one another and relative to money.

(ix) The gross total of wealth. This is the constraint within which households and firms have to allocate their total assets between money and non-monetary assets.

The use of money as a means of payment, and its role as an asset, are *both* necessary to an understanding of the relevance to the demand for money of the variables listed above. Recognition of the interdependence of the payments function and the asset role of money has come slowly during the present century. Alfred Marshall argued that motives with respect to both 'convenience' and 'security' influence the demand for money; and his emphasis on money as an asset was followed up by later economists at the University of Cambridge. In particular, Keynes put the asset role of money in the forefront of the analysis in both his major works [26, 27].

In the *General Theory,* Keynes distinguishes three motives – the transactions, the precautionary and the speculative – for holding money ([27] chap. 15). He usually considered the former two together, and this has led to the standard textbook division of the demand for money into two parts – a transactions demand and an asset demand. This does not seem to be a useful distinction since money and other assets are substitutes in respect of all intended lengths of holding period for wealth. The degree of substitutability will, of course, vary with the length of the holding period. But *all* the influences on the demand for money (e.g. all those which Keynes grouped under his three motives) are relevant to each length of holding period. Their relative importance will be different from period to period. But this is a matter of degree, and not one that permits a clear-cut division of the demand for money into different parts – as Keynes himself recognised ([27] p. 195).

This conclusion has been supported from a number of angles in the literature. So-called transactions balances will vary with changes in interest rates since these are opportunity costs of holding money [1, 42]. But since it is expectations about interest rates that are relevant in this respect, the speculative motive comes into the picture. Moreover, since speculation about future interest rates brings in the uncertainties attaching to expectations, a precautionary motive has also to be taken into account [43]. Thus, both a speculative (or expectational) element and a precautionary (or risk-averting) element enter into the choices between money and other assets. But, in addition, those choices depend upon the expectations about the prices of the goods that wealth can be used to acquire in the future [9]. Hence, speculation and precaution in regard to *all* future prices influence the demand for money.

It is clear therefore that the theory of the demand for money must be seen as part of a much wider theory – that of 'portfolio selection'. This was first clearly expressed by Hicks [19]. At any moment of time a wealth-owner has to decide upon the proportions of his total assets that he will put into different forms – for example into money, deposits with non-bank financial intermediaries, bonds with different maturity dates, shares and durable goods. These assets will yield services of various kinds, both pecuniary and non-pecuniary, and the expected amounts of the services can be expressed as rates of return on the assets. To optimise his position, a wealth-owner will select a 'portfolio' of assets in which the *marginal* rates of return are equal on all the assets held. This condition ensures that he cannot improve his position by holding more of one asset and less of another.

But these are *expected* rates of return and are therefore subject to uncertainties. The latter could be expressed by means of individual assessments of the chances that the return on a particular asset will diverge, either above or below, from its most probable expected value. To illustrate this simply, suppose that a person expects a bond to yield a 5% return in six cases out of ten, but expects that the return will be 4% in two cases out of ten and will be 6% in two cases out of ten. The expected returns are dispersed (normally, in this example) around a mean of 5%. The dispersion could be taken as a measure of the uncertainty attaching to the most probable outcome of 5%. The larger this dispersion is, the more uncertain the person is about the rate of return he will get on the bond.

In selecting between two assets for which the most probable rates of return are the *same*, a risk-averter will choose the one with the smaller degree of uncertainty, i.e. the one for which the dispersion of expected returns around the mean is the smaller. More generally, in selecting a whole portfolio of assets he will have to achieve a balance between the mean expectations and their degrees of uncertainty (as indicated by some measure of dispersion) for all assets. This can be expressed by saying that he will select a portfolio in which the marginal rates of return, *adjusted for risk*, are equal on all the assets held ([21] chap. 2).

The theory of portfolio selection has been elaborated by Tobin [45] and others at Yale University. It shows that the explanation of the demand for money is likely to be a complex one, since any well-developed financial system confronts wealth-owners with a great range and variety of assets from which to select. This conclusion accords with the long list of variables, analysed above, that may influence the demand for money. Nevertheless, it may be that a few of these variables are, in some sense, the most important ones.

Thus some economists, and in particular Gurley and Shaw ([18] chap. 6), have argued that the liabilities of non-bank financial intermediaries are especially close substitutes for money. This view was accepted, and broadened, by the Radcliffe Committee ([39] chap. 6) in its argument that the demand for money must be analysed as part of the demand for a whole range of 'liquid' assets.

The 'liquidity' of an asset is a complex concept since it involves at least two sets of characteristics. The first is sometimes called the 'marketability' of an asset, in the sense of the ease with which a holder of it could obtain the highest price that anyone else is willing to pay. This is basically a matter of transactions costs, which will depend, *inter alia*, on the number of individuals wishing to purchase the asset during any period of time, and on the market organisation for the dissemination of information [34]. The more perfect is a market, the smaller will be the transactions costs incurred in finding the highest bidder for an asset, and the greater will be the liquidity of the asset.

The second aspect of liquidity concerns the degree of uncertainty attaching to the price at which an asset can be sold. The smaller is that uncertainty, the more liquid is the asset. Uncertainty depends in part on the terms to maturity of an asset. A short-term bond is more liquid than a long-term one, since the price of the former will be altered less by a given change in market interest rates (see [31] chap. 3, for the mathematics of bond-price movements). But the whole state of expectations, which is dependent on the chances of disturbances in particular markets or in the economy in general, helps to determine the liquidity of assets. Thus the liquidity of all non-monetary assets will be reduced by an increase in the chances that many individuals will want to sell them at the same time.

Liquid assets are, by definition, close substitutes for money. But liquidity is a matter of degree. The fixed-price liabilities of non-bank financial intermediaries are highly liquid even taking into account that they cannot be encashed immediately. So also

23

may be various very short-term negotiable financial instruments. But there is no clear-cut, and fixed, dividing line between liquid and non-liquid assets ([15] chap. 3). Hence the attempt to simplify the demand for money function, by concentrating attention on the substitution relations between money and liquid assets, seems unlikely to be useful.

It is possible, however, to approach the question of simplification from another angle. Thus Friedman argues that the choices between money and *all* other assets can be explained in terms of a small number of variables. In common with other contemporary monetary theorists, he regards the demand for money as a problem belonging to the theory of portfolio selection or, as he usually puts it, to capital theory. But it is essential to notice the differences, as between Friedman and others, in the emphases put on the various elements in the analysis.

For Friedman, the quantity demanded of money (measured in real terms) depends mainly on wealth, the expected (average) rate of return on bonds, the expected (average) rate of return on shares (taken to include durable goods), the expected rate of change of goods prices, and individual preferences between different forms of wealth [9]. Since wealth is the capitalised value of expected future incomes, a measure for the latter (called 'permanent' income by Friedman) could be substituted for wealth in his demand function.

The derivation of this function is explained mainly in terms of the asset role of money, with little attention being given to the details of the payments function of money. The relevance of transactions costs, and of different holding periods for wealth, for the demands for different kinds of assets is not investigated. Or put another way, the nature of the services provided by money balances is not enquired into closely. Rather, the analysis proceeds on a more abstract level. All assets – money, bonds, shares, durable goods – provide services which yield rates of return on them. For each individual, the rate of return on any asset will diminish as his holding of it increases. Each individual will allocate his wealth between different assets so as to equalise their marginal rates of return. If the latter are not equal, there will be a re-allocation of wealth between *all* assets.

Friedman's theory of the demand for money seems to imply

24

close substitutability between all forms of wealth – money, financial and real assets. But it does so without a detailed analysis of the reasons for substitutability between different kinds of asset. In particular, it pays little attention to the questions of transactions costs, different holding periods for wealth and risk aversion. As a result, the number of variables in the argument of Friedman's demand for money function is smaller than that in the function derived at an earlier stage above.

It may still be true, of course, that Friedman's function includes all the variables which are, in some sense, the most important for the demand for money. Whether or not that is so can only, as Friedman emphasises, be demonstrated by reference to the facts. But the function of a theory is to propound clear questions for answer from the facts. It is therefore necessary to enquire into the precise meaning of an assertion that the quantity demanded of money can be explained in terms of a small number of variables.

Three aspects of this matter must be distinguished, namely (1) the sizes of the coefficients relating the quantity demanded of money to the independent variables in the demand for money function, (2) the determination of the independent variables themselves, and (3) any time lags that exist in relation to the demand for money.

(1) A quantified form of the demand for money function would show the magnitudes of the effects on the quantity demanded of money of changes in the independent variables that determine it. For example, it would indicate by how much the quantity demanded would rise if there is an increase in the level of incomes, and by how much it would fall if there is an increase in the level of interest rates. These quantitative relationships can be expressed by means of elasticities, e.g. the interest-elasticity of the demand for money.

The sizes of the elasticities, in respect of all the independent variables, might be taken as measures of the relative importance of these variables for the demand for money. If it is thought that a particular elasticity is quite small, then it might be judged that, as a first approximation, the independent variable in question could be dropped from the demand for money function. In this way, the number of variables in the argument of that function might be reduced to a smaller number. There is in fact some dispute about the size of the interest-elasticity of the demand for money; and we know very little about the quantitive relation between the demand for money and transactions costs. It follows therefore that different specifications of the demand for money function can be the result of different economists' views on the sizes of the relevant elasticities.

(2) But the matter does not rest there. The importance of a particular variable for the demand for money does not depend solely on the size of the elasticity in question. It also depends on the degree of variability in the variable itself. For example, even if the interest-elasticity of the demand for money were quite small, interest rates could be important for the demand for money if they were subject to large variations whenever the equilibrium of an economy is disturbed.

It is necessary therefore, in deciding which are the important variables for the demand for money, to know how these variables are themselves determined. But that depends on the complete working of the economy since all its parts are mutually interdependent. Hence the demand for the money function has to be specified in the context of *all* the functional relations in the macro-economic model of the price system.

Expectations (e.g. of incomes and interest rates) are the most troublesome element in this respect. We do not know much about how they are formed. Little progress has yet been made in specifying the functions which explain the formation of expectations. Hence the importance attached to expectations (and their uncertainties) in relation to the demand for money depends on economists' intuitions as to their degree of variability. The significance of this point will be taken up in Section 6 below.

(3) The demand for money function may be made more complex by the existence of time lags. Suppose that expectations with respect to incomes, interest rates and rates of return of real assets are all based in some way on their past values. The paths taken by the latter through time will determine the formation of expectations from period to period, which, in their turn, will determine the demand for money. But all the variables in question will act and react on one another in this process. The values taken by

them will depend on that interaction, and therefore on the structure of the time lags involved (as can be seen in dynamic macro-economic models).

Moreover, the demand for money may depend not only on lags in the formation of expectations, but also on lags in the adjustment of portfolios to their desired sizes and composition. Because of the time and effort involved in making and executing decisions, individuals review their portfolios only from time to time. Financial institutions do this at very short intervals, but these are much longer for most households.

Time lags, the sizes of the elasticities with respect to the independent variables and the degree of variability in the latter must all be taken into account in judging an assertion that the quantity demanded of money can be explained in terms of a small number of variables. As has been seen, this raises issues that can be dealt with only later when the demand for money function is put into a complete macro-economic model.

4 The Supply of Money

Money was provisionally defined, in Section 2 above, so as to comprise coin, bank notes and demand deposits at commercial banks. On this basis, an explanation of what determines the quantity supplied of money requires an analysis of the behaviour of commercial banks and of the central bank which has overall control of the banking sector.

It is essential to have a clear understanding at the outset of what is entailed by this enquiry. The objective is to construct a supply of money function that specifies the variables which determine the quantity supplied of money. By the 'quantity supplied' is meant the quantity of money which the banking system would be *willing* to create in given circumstances. That 'willingness' is dependent on the variables in the argument of the supply function.

The quantity supplied must not be confused with the quantity of money in existence – just as the quantity demanded of money must not be confused with the quantity actually held. The quantity of money in existence at any moment depends on *both* the supply and the demand functions for money, i.e. on both the willingness of the banks to create money and the willingness of the community to hold it. Once the supply function is constructed, its interaction with the demand function can be taken up in Section 5 below.

The danger of confusion in these respects arises from the usual introductory-textbook account of the 'bank-credit multiplier'. This is a supply-oriented analysis of the creation of money in which the holding of money is taken as a passive affair. Moreover the credit multiplier is usually presented as the result of the maintenance by commercial banks of certain more or less fixed ratios between their assets – and particularly as the outcome of their obligation to keep to a given cash ratio. But the proportions in which banks wish to hold various kinds of assets need to be explained. Normally commercial banks are privately-owned, profit-seeking institutions. Both the total assets they hold, and their composition, will be the result of their attempts to maximise profits within any legal or customary constraints placed on their operation. That is the context in which the supply of money has to be explained.

The liabilities of commercial banks are predominantly the demand and time deposits of their customers; issued capital and reserves are a very small fraction of total liabilities. Their assets typically comprise cash (coin and notes held plus a deposit at the central bank); highly 'liquid' assets like very short-term loans to households and firms; and short-term government securities. Real assets (buildings and equipment) are a very small fraction of total assets. Commercial banks are one kind of financial intermediary; their business centres on borrowing and lending. Whether or not they are clearly distinguishable – by the fact that some of their liabilities are money – from other (non-bank) financial intermediaries will be considered later.

The behaviour of banks can be analysed in terms of the theory of portfolio selection. To maximise profits, the composition of their assets must be such that the marginal rates of return (interest) on all kinds of them are equal. If they are not equal, a bank could increase its profits by substituting, to some extent, a higher-yield for a lower-yield asset. The return on each asset must take into account any expected change in its price over the intended holding period; and it must be computed net of transactions costs because these are likely to differ from asset to asset. Since the expected prices of assets cannot be certain, and since banks are probably risk-averters, they will make an allowance for risk in the expected returns on assets. They will aim to equalise marginal rates of return *adjusted for risk*. Thus the diversification of the assets held by banks can be explained in the same way as for households or non-bank firms.

The same is true of their holding of cash. For banks, cash (coin, notes and a deposit at the central bank) is the only kind of money they can use to clear their own debts. Obviously they cannot use bank money (bank liabilities) to settle bank liabilities.

29

But the banks' demand for cash is explained in exactly the same way as the rest of the community's demand for money in general. The prospective receipts and payments of banks are unlikely to be synchronised perfectly over time. They will therefore want to hold some cash in the time intervals between receipts and payments. How much will depend on the expected levels of the latter, on transactions costs, and on the expected rates of return (and their uncertainties) on the other assets that could be held instead of cash.

It follows therefore that the variables in the arguments of the banks' demand for cash functions are of the same nature as those in the arguments of households' and non-bank firms' demand for money functions. Two consequences of this need to be noticed. First, the larger is the total of assets held by banks, the greater will be their receipts and payments during any period of time. Hence the banks' demand for cash will increase as the desired total of their assets rises. Second, the banks' demand for cash will decrease (given their total assets) as the expected rates of return on other assets rise – since the latter are the opportunity costs of holding cash. In other words, the banks' *desired ratio* between cash and total assets will fall as the rates of interest on their lending rise.

This conclusion about the desired *composition* of bank assets has implications for the *total* of their assets and therefore for the supply of money. Suppose that the quantity of cash *available* to the banks is given and constant, and that there are no legal or customary constraints on their cash ratios. Then as interest rates rise, the banks will be willing to increase their lending since they are ready to reduce the ratio between cash and other assets. Banks lend by offering demand deposits in exchange for the liabilities of households, firms and the government. An increase in the supply of bank lending means an increase in the supply of money. Hence, in the assumed circumstances, the quantity supplied of money would increase as interest rates rise.

But commercial banks usually have to observe some form of minimum cash ratio (laid down by law, or at the behest of the central bank). If interest rates are such as to make the desired cash ratio equal to the minimum permitted ratio, then a rise in interest rates (which lowers the desired ratio) can have no effect on the supply of bank lending and of money. The minimum cash ratio acts as a constraint on the profit-maximising behaviour of the banks. But if the desired cash ratio is above the minimum level (i.e. the banks are holding 'excess' cash reserves), the quantity supplied of money will increase to some extent in response to a rise in interest rates.

It is now necessary to ask how the quantity of cash available to the commercial banks is determined. This depends on portfolio decisions in the rest of the economy, in ways that need careful examination.

Commercial banks acquire their portfolios of assets by offering their own liabilities in exchange. The sellers of bonds to the banks, or the recipients of bank loans, receive additions to their demand deposits. But each possessor of a demand deposit is free to choose how to hold this portion of his wealth. He could decide to exchange it for cash, or for time deposits, or for other financial assets, or for real assets. His portfolio decision will have different effects on the banks in each of these cases.

If he exchanges the demand deposit for cash, the banks will lose cash. If the exchange is for a time deposit, the composition of bank liabilities will be altered; and there will be a consequential effect on their total if the cash ratio in respect of time deposits is different from that for demand deposits. If he exchanges the demand deposit for other financial assets, or for real assets, it will pass into someone else's portfolio. The latter might be a household, a non-financial firm, or a non-bank financial intermediary – or the central bank. If it is not the central bank which sells the asset in question, the transaction will not affect the commercial banks' holding of cash. There will merely be a change in the ownership of bank liabilities. But if the central bank acquires the demand deposit, by selling an asset from its portfolio, the commercial banks will lose cash, i.e. their deposits at the central bank will fall. (The whole of this, and the following, analysis ignores budgetary and balance of payments complications, for which space cannot be made.)

It follows that the quantity of cash available to the commercial banks depends on the portfolio decisions of both the non-bank public and the central bank. But, as regards the former, it is decisions in two respects only that matter, namely (i) on the choice between cash (coin plus bank notes) and *all* other assets taken together, and (ii) on the choice between demand and time deposits, where, however, this is relevant only if the banks' cash ratios differ for the two types of deposit. Leaving (ii) aside, it is the public's decision only on how much cash to hold that can affect the cash reserves of the banks. Their portfolio decisions as between all other assets – including demand deposits – are not relevant in this aspect. If they decide to substitute other assets (except cash) for demand deposits, this leads merely to a redistribution in the ownership of the latter. In particular, it should be noted that a decision by the public to hold more of the liabilities of non-bank financial intermediaries will cause an increase in the demand deposits held by these intermediaries.

The public's demand for cash places a constraint on the quantity supplied of demand deposits. As the latter increases, the public will probably want to hold more cash in order to maintain equilibrium within its portfolios. Therefore, in drawing additional cash out of the banks, it will constrain the total of lending that the banks can undertake.

It is the *total* of assets owned by the central bank that helps to determine the quantity of cash available to the commercial banks. An increase in that total (through open-market operations) will raise the cash reserves of the banks, and vice versa. The prime function of a central bank is to carry out the monetary policy of a country and is not that of maximising profit. The total of its assets will therefore depend on its pursuit of the country's economic objectives.

THE SUPPLY FUNCTION

As with the demand function, it will be helpful to summarise the variables that enter into the argument of the supply of money function ([3] chap. 1).

The *nominal* quantity supplied of money depends on :

(i) The desired cash-to-total-assets ratios of the commercial banks. This is only a summary way of referring to all the variables which appear in their demand for cash functions.

(ii) Legal or customary minima for the banks' cash ratios. These may or may not be effective constraints at any time.

(iii) The desired cash-to-total-assets ratios of the non-bank public. These are one aspect of the public's overall portfolio preferences.

(iv) The desired demand-deposit-to-time-deposit ratios of the public, whenever the banks' cash ratios differ for these two types of deposit.

(v) The central bank's desired total of assets. This depends on its various policy objectives.

The theory of the supply of money has been improved by the application to it of the principles of portfolio selection. These explain how, with a constant total of assets held by the central bank, the supply of money may still increase or decrease in response to changes in the economy. This will happen, for example, when changes in the expected rates of return on assets, and in their degrees of uncertainty, cause either the banks or the public to alter their cash-to-total-assets ratios; or again, when a change in the level of national income causes the public to hold less or more cash to meet everyday expenditures. Moreover – as with the demand for money – time lags in the formation of expectations, and in the adjustment of portfolios, will have to be taken into account in explaining the supply of money.

The behaviour of the money supply depends also on the total assets held by the central bank. It is essential to distinguish, in this respect, what a central bank *actually* does from what it *could* do. Central banks undoubtedly do vary the money supply in response to changes in the economy, though probably not according to any simple set of rules. The supply of money therefore depends – though in a complex way – on the level of economic activity. This has to be borne in mind in any interpretation of monetary statistics.

But this does not mean that a central bank could not control the money supply at any level that it wishes. It can always do that by an appropriate variation in the total of its assets. However, as will be seen in the next section, the supply of money helps to determine the level of interest rates. Hence a central bank is faced with a choice between fixing *either* the money supply *or* the level of interest rates. It cannot do both. If it chooses to determine the level of interest rates, it loses control over the supply of money which must then accord with what the public wants to hold at the interest-rate level in question. This fact was sometimes forgotten in the dispute, since the mid-1950s, as to whether the Bank of England is able to control the U.K. money supply by operations on the cash reserves of the commercial banks [7].

It is particularly in the understanding of the interrelations of commercial banks and non-bank financial intermediaries that the theory of portfolio selection has had an important role. Non-bank financial intermediaries (NBFIs) aim, just like banks, to have portfolios of different assets in which the expected marginal rates of return, adjusted for risk, are all equal. One of these assets is money balances, mainly in the form of demand deposits at commercial banks. The NBFIs' demand for money depends on the same kind of variables as have already been set out in general terms. They will therefore want to hold larger money balances, the greater are the totals of their assets; but they will be willing to hold smaller money balances – at any level of total assets – the higher are the expected rates of return on their other assets. That is, their *desired* money-to-total-assets ratios will fall as those expected returns rise. As contrasted with banks, these ratios are often not subject to legal minima.

The amount of money balances *available* to the NBFIs, and their desired money-to-total-assets ratios, determine the quantity of loans they are willing to supply. They will lend (i.e. acquire assets) up to the level at which their demand for money balances (as given by their desired money-to-total-assets ratios) is equal to the amount of money they hold. Now the latter depends on the portfolio decisions of the public; and in particular on its decisions on the choice between NBFI liabilities and *all* other assets. The larger the amount of NBFI liabilities that the public wants to hold relative to other assets, the greater will be the transfer of demand deposits from the public to the NBFIs, and therefore the greater will be the supply of NBFI loans.

Hence, the latter is constrained by the amount of demand deposits which the public wishes to hold out of the quantity supplied of them by the commercial banks. And, as has been seen, the supply of bank deposits is constrained by the amount of cash which the public wishes to hold out of the quantity supplied of it

34

by the central bank. We have here, as it were, an inverted pyramid of 'credit'. The central bank provides the cash reserves needed for commercial bank lending; and the commercial banks provide the money reserves needed for NBFI lending. But throughout the system, the public's portfolio decisions, as between cash, demand deposits, NBFI liabilities and other assets, help to determine the amounts of reserves available to all the financial intermediaries (including banks) – and therefore help to determine the supply of loans by all of the latter.

This analysis leads to the conclusion that there is not a sharp distinction between commercial banks and NBFIs. It is sometimes argued that the former are in a unique position, as regards the 'creation of credit', because their demand liabilities are money [50]. This seems to be mistaken. Bank liabilities and NBFI liabilities are substitutes; and the supply of loans by NBFIs depends on the willingness of the public to hold their liabilities (rather than other assets), just as the supply of bank loans depends on the willingness of the public to hold bank liabilities (rather than cash). The differences between NBFIs and banks are one of degree [44]; and that turns very much on the degree of substitutability between their liabilities [41].

5 Monetary Dynamics

If the quantity demanded of money is not equal to the quantity supplied, this means that the portfolios of some households and/or firms (including financial ones) are not in equilibrium. Either the quantity of money in existence is not equal to the amount that the community wants to hold in the given circumstances, or the actual quantity is not equal to the amount that the banking system wants to supply, or both of these conditions.

An enquiry into the consequences of this monetary disequilibrium is an exercise in dynamic analysis. It is an attempt to trace the paths which will be followed by the variables that are disturbed by the disequilibrium. It has an analogue in the Marshallian period analysis of changes in the price and output of a single good. But since money ramifies the whole working of an economy, the analysis of monetary disequilibrium requires a complete model of the economy such as one of those constructed in macro-economics.

A short monograph must practise some division of labour in that respect; and this will be done as follows. Monetary disequilibrium will lead to changes in portfolios, and these will probably affect the aggregate demand for currently-produced goods and services which helps to determine the levels of national output and prices. In the present section, the analysis will concentrate on those portfolio changes and the consequential effects on aggregate demand. It will not be possible to ignore entirely the changes in national output and prices that may follow, since these will have 'feedback' effects on portfolios. But as far as possible the discussion of the effects on output and prices of monetary disequilibrium will be held back to the final section. However, that discussion will be only of a selective nature since a comprehensive macro-economic analysis cannot be undertaken.

Monetary disequilibrium will result from a change in *any* of the variables in the arguments of the demand or the supply functions for money. Such a change alters the quantity demanded or the quantity supplied of money and therefore disrupts an equilibrium between the two. But the change in question may have other 'impact' effects on the economy as well as the disturbance of monetary equilibrium. For example, a rise in the expected rates of return on real assets will not only increase the demand for money – to carry out additional expenditures on investment – it will also increase the aggregate demand for national output. It is obviously necessary to take both these impact effects into account in analysing the consequences of the change in question.

In general, it is essential to specify very carefully the cause of any monetary disequilibrium in order to ensure that all its impact effects are allowed for. Different causes in this respect are likely to have different sets of impact effects, and monetary analysis must distinguish between them. It is possible, in the space available here, only to work through the likely consequences of one kind of monetary disturbance. But it has been chosen so that the analysis will also provide the principles for enquiry into other types of disturbance.

The one chosen is an increase in the quantity supplied of money as a result of central bank action. It is immediately necessary, as indicated above, to specify all the impact effects of this action. Consider a number of possibilities:

(i) The central bank purchases securities in the open market, thereby increasing the cash reserves of the commercial banks which makes them willing to supply more demand deposits.

(ii) The central bank provides the government with more demand deposits to enable it to finance a budget deficit.

(iii) The central bank increases the supply of money, through open-market operations, in order to provide the finance for an increase in the rate of investment which the private sector wishes to undertake because of an improvement in prospective profits.

The impact effects of (ii) and (iii) are different from those of (i). In the former two there is an increase in the desire to spend (by government or firms) *as well as* an increase in the supply of money. In the latter there is an increase *only* in the supply of

37

money. The difference in impact effects can be put in terms of a distinction between an *income effect* and a *substitution effect*.

An increase in the desire to spend by government or firms means an increase in the aggregate demand for goods; the impact of this is an income effect. An increase in the supply of money is an offer, by the banks, of demand deposits in exchange for securities held by the public; the impact of this is a substitution effect on the portfolios of the public. There are both income and substitution effects in (ii) and (iii) above; but only a substitution effect in (i). Of course, the substitution effect (in all three cases) may have consequences – e.g. a change in interest rates – that will affect the community's desire to spend on goods. But those consequences must not be confused with other causes of an increase in the desire to spend (e.g. the improvement in prospective profits in (ii) above).

The initial open-market purchase of securities by the central bank, and the resulting increase in the supply of demand deposits by commercial banks in exchange for securities, will probably raise the market prices of those securities (at least in case (i) above). The individuals who have sold them, and those who still retain some of them in their portfolios, will have had an increase in the market value of their assets. This is a *wealth effect* of an increase in the supply of money.

Knowledge of the fact that the central bank is increasing the money supply may influence the expectations of firms and households. Some of them may think, rightly or wrongly, that the change in monetary policy will have effects on the levels of national output and prices. This is an *expectations effect* of an increase in the supply of money.

The impact of a change in the quantity supplied of money may be some combination of income, substitution, wealth and expectations effects. The consequences of the substitution effect are the most difficult to analyse, and they will be considered first.

CHANGE IN THE MONEY SUPPLY

It has been emphasised earlier that the quantity of money in existence depends on the interaction of the demand and the supply functions for money. When the central bank wants to increase the quantity of money, through open-market operations, it must persuade the holders of securities to sell them to it in return for demand deposits. It does this by bidding up security prices, and therefore lowering the market interest rates on them. Central banks usually operate at the short end of the securities market, by dealing in bills or very short-term bonds, but they may also on occasion deal in longer-dated bonds. The immediate effect of their market purchases is therefore usually to reduce short-term interest rates. This is reinforced by similar purchases on the part of the commercial banks whose cash reserves have been increased.

The fall in short-term interest rates makes it more attractive to hold money (because an opportunity cost of so doing has fallen) and also more attractive to hold longer-dated bonds (whose interest rates have not fallen). Hence some of the proceeds, from the sales of securities to the banks, will now be used to purchase longer-dated bonds. Their prices will rise and thus the fall in short-term interest rates will spread to medium- and long-term rates. This process can be reinforced by the central bank purchasing longer-dated as well as shorter-dated bonds.

But the desired substitutions of *both* money and longer-dated bonds, for the short-term securities sold to the banks, will depend on expectations about future bond prices (i.e. interest rates). This point has already been referred to on p. 16 above. *Given* individuals' bond-price expectations – which will differ to some extent from one another – a rise in current bond prices will make *more* individuals bearish about the future. This will increase the demand for money. Moreover these bearish sentiments will militate against the purchase of longer-dated bonds.

The choice between short- and long-term bonds, for any given holding period, depends on a comparison between the returns expected to be earned on them over that period. Either a succession of short-term bonds can be held over the period or a single long-term bond. The return on the former will be made up of the current short-term interest rate on the first bond held plus the expected interest rates on the succeeding bonds. The return on a long-term bond will be made up of the current long-term interest rate plus or minus any expected change in the price of the bond over the period in question (which is given by the expected change in the long-term interest rate). Thus the choice between short- and long-term bonds depends on expectations about future interest rates; and probably also on the uncertainties attaching to these expectations. This whole matter is dealt with in the theory of the term structure of interest rates [31].

Return now to the fall in short-term interest rates which was being considered above. Assume again that interest-rate (bond price) expectations are given. Then those expectations will determine the extent to which people will buy longer-dated bonds with the proceeds from their sales of short-term securities to the banks. The more bearish is the community, the less it will be ready to buy longer-dated bonds, and therefore the smaller will be the fall in long-term interest rates as a result of the increase in the supply of money.

But interest-rate expectations are unlikely to remain unchanged in this situation. As time goes on, the experience of lower interest rates will lead to a revision of expectations. In particular, those (the bears) who had been expecting interest rates to be higher will find their expectations disappointed and are likely to adjust them in a downward direction. That is, expectations will be formed in the light of the errors in previous predictions ([33] chap. 2). There will, however, be time lags in this process of learning from the experience of forecasting-errors.

The downward adjustment in interest-rate expectations will now increase the demand for longer-dated bonds (i.e. decrease the demand for money). The consequent fall in long-term interest rates will be subject to time lags in the adjustment of portfolios (which are additional to the time lags in the formation of expectations; see p. 27 above). Both sets of lags will be the shorter, the more important is the role of financial institutions in credit markets, since they specialise in choosing portfolios.

It is essential to notice that the portion of the new demand deposits (created by the central bank action), which is used to purchase longer-dated bonds, will be circulating from individual to individual during those purchases. These deposits will rest with particular individuals only for as long as it takes them to make up their minds to acquire bonds rather than to hold money. Hence the increase in the *demand* to hold money balances (on

40

average over a period of time) will depend on the length of the time lags in question.

Some of these bank deposits will be acquired by NBFIs. As interest rates on marketable securities fall, the liabilities of the NBFIs become relatively more attractive to hold. The community increases its holding of those liabilities by transferring demand deposits to the NBFIs [16]. The rise in their money balances increases their willingness to lend and therefore lowers the interest rates on that lending [47].

Moreover, the general fall in interest rates will, in itself, also make the holding of shares relatively more attractive. The demand for shares depends on the expected rates of return on them, and their degrees of uncertainty, relative to those on other assets. The expected returns on shares depend, in their turn, on the community's expectations about the profitability of the firms that issued them. If those profit expectations remain unchanged, then a fall in interest rates will increase the demand for shares since they are now relatively more attractive than bonds. That will raise share prices and lower the expected rates of return on them. But any increase in the demand for shares will be subject to the time lags (in respect of interest-rate expectations and portfolio adjustments) considered above. Now it is quite possible for profit expectations to change during the operation of those lags. If they were to deteriorate, this would offset, to some extent, the effect of the fall in interest rates. That is, the demand for shares – and therefore their prices – would not rise as much (if at all) as would otherwise have been the case. In general, it is not possible to say how share prices will be affected by a change in interest rates unless it is also known what is happening concurrently to the expected profitability of firms.

The analysis of the substitution effects, following upon an increase in the supply of money, which has been confined so far to those between money and financial assets, must now be extended to include real assets. These can yield services in a variety of forms: consumption services to households owning consumer durable goods, production services to firms using producer durable goods and, more generally, the service of any durable good as a means of storing wealth through time. It has already been argued (on p. 15 above) that, in the latter respect, money

41

and most durable goods are only distant substitutes; and the same is true for most financial assets and durable goods. High transaction and storage costs, and the need for specialised knowledge, militate against the holding of most real assets merely as a store of value between receipts and intended payments. Hence when the rates of return on financial assets fall, it is unlikely that households and firms will want to hold significantly higher proportions of their *existing* total assets in the form of durable goods. They may, however, want, in these circumstances, to *add* to their total assets at a more rapid rate.

The rates of return on existing financial assets determine the costs of financing additions to total assets. Firms and households, who borrow in order to purchase real assets, must pay the going rates of interest; and firms, that issue shares to the same end, must offer prospects of rates of return on them which are comparable to those on existing shares. These costs of finance have to be set against the expected rates of return (and their degrees of uncertainty) on the real assets that may be acquired with the finance, i.e. against the expected profits on new capital goods in the case of firms, and against the subjective valuations of the services from new consumer durables in the case of households. Given the latter expected rates of return, a fall in the costs of finance will probably induce individuals to add more rapidly, than they had previously desired, to their stocks of real assets. That is, the substitution effects, following from an increase in the supply of money, will lead to an increase in the rate of investment by both firms and households.

The desire to *add* to the stock of real assets provides one link between portfolio decisions and expenditure decisions with respect to currently-produced goods. The substitution effects behind this link are often referred to as the 'interest-rate mechanism'. But it is necessary to interpret that term in a wide sense. On the one hand, it refers to the whole range of financial liabilities that can be newly issued (or sold out of existing holdings) to finance the acquisition of real assets. 'Interest rate' therefore encompasses a spectrum of interest rates on loans of different kinds and of different terms to maturity; and it also includes the expected rates of return on shares that will be sufficient to induce people to purchase them. On the other hand, real assets cover all types of durable goods including consumer durables as well as the fixed capital and inventories of firms.

It is essential to remember that the interest-rate mechanism involves not only the expected rates of return on financial assets, but also the expected rates of return on real assets. The rate of investment will be affected when the former change *relatively* to the latter. Thus a fall in the absolute level of interest rates will stimulate investment only if the expected returns on real assets do not fall simultaneously to the same extent.

The latter depend on firms' expectations about their future sales of goods and on consumers' expectations about their future levels of income. These expectations are formed in the light of recent experience of sales and incomes, which are determined by current expenditure levels.

It follows that the interest-rate mechanism, linking portfolio decisions and current expenditure decisions, involves mutual interdependence between its two sides. The relation between interest rates and expected returns on real assets helps to determine the level of investment, which is one constituent of current expenditure on goods. But the level of the latter helps to determine the expected returns on real assets, which is one element in portfolio decisions.

There are time lags at work on both sides of this mechanism. Those in the formation of interest-rate expectations, and in the adjustment of portfolios, have already been noticed. A further one, in relation to portfolio adjustment, must now be introduced. Financial institutions do not alter their interest rates continuously so as to maintain equality between the quantities demanded and supplied of loans at all times. There are various reasons for this lag in the adjustment of interest rates to their equilibrium levels, e.g. the administrative costs of making frequent changes, uncertainty, lack of competition, and institutional arrangements with the central bank. Moreover, financial institutions are confronted by borrowers who have different degrees of creditworthiness. The institutions may therefore, to their own advantage, alter the amount of their lending, not by changing interest rates, but by varying the degree of creditworthiness that they will countenance in borrowers at any time

[22]. When they are in a position to lend more they may lower the required standard of creditworthiness, at given interest rates, and vice versa.

For these various reasons, there will be excess demand for, or excess supply of, loans at existing interest rates which have not been adjusted to their equilibrium levels. This modifies the operation of the interest-rate mechanism. The *availability* of loans, as well as the *price* of loans (the interest rate), can now affect the level of current expenditure on goods. Thus, when there is excess demand for loans at ruling interest rates, current expenditure will be curtailed by the 'rationing' of loans. An increase in the supply of money, in this situation, can therefore lead to some rise in lending, and therefore in current expenditure, without a fall in interest rates.

The rise in the prices of existing financial assets, as a result of an increase in the supply of money, means that those assets are now worth more in terms of currently-produced consumer goods and services. In that sense the holders of the assets have enjoyed an increase in their wealth. This is a wealth effect – which is additional to the substitution effects – of an increase in the supply of money. But this change in asset prices is not accompanied by any change in the sizes of the future incomes that will flow from those assets. It is the *ratio* between asset prices and the prospective incomes from them that has been altered by the fall in the interest rates – not the absolute amounts of interest that can be earned from them. Hence the owners of the assets are no better off in terms of the current and future incomes that they will get from them.

Nevertheless, a rise in asset prices (as a result of a fall in interest rates) may make individuals 'feel richer' and may therefore lead them to spend more on consumption, i.e. to increase their consumption-to-income ratios. Of course, in doing so, they reduce the quantities of assets they could have had in the future, and therefore reduce the amount of consumption they can undertake in the future. This wealth effect on consumption expenditure – called the Keynes-effect because of the importance he attached to it ([27] chap. 8) – will therefore depend on individuals' preferences as between present and future consumption in relation to the current values of assets and the prospective incomes from

44

them (this somewhat complicated matter is analysed in [29] chap. 4).

The Keynes-effect must not be confused with another possible effect on consumption expenditure of a change in interest rates. A fall in interest rates raises the the prices of future goods relatively to present goods, since larger sums have to be set aside to accumulate at interest towards the purchase of goods in the future. For this reason, individuals may substitute present goods for future goods, i.e. they may consume more (save less) as interest rates fall. This was the 'classical' explanation of the relation between saving and the interest rate.

There is one more possible effect of an increase in the supply of money to take into account. Knowledge of this change in monetary policy may lead some firms and households to reason that the level of economic activity will therefore rise. The consequential improvement in profit and income expectations will increase expenditures on investment and consumption. But the operation of this expectations effect depends on a firm belief both in the efficacy of the monetary change and in the monetary authority's willingness to sustain it.

RESTORATION OF EQUILIBRIUM

The whole analysis above can now be rounded off by a review of the ways in which monetary equilibrium is restored. The increase in the supply of money will continue to cause changes in the economy until the quantity demanded of money has risen to equality with the new quantity supplied. As long as there is an excess supply of money, either the banking system, if it is not supplying as much as it wants to, or the public, if it is holding more money balances that it wishes to, or both, will continue to adjust their portfolios. It is through these adjustments of portfolios that the increase in the supply of money works its effects on the economy.

To restore monetary equilibrium, these effects must change at least some of the variables in the argument of the demand for money function so as to increase the quantity demanded of money. It is suggested that the reader might like to refresh his memory of the list of these variables (on p. 20 above), bearing in mind, however, that the analysis has yet to consider (in the next section) how an increase in current expenditure will affect the levels of national output and/or prices. This should help him to see more precisely how the substitution, wealth and expectations effects of an increase in the supply of money can cause a rise in the quantity demanded of money. It will be assumed here that there are no direct income effects of the increased supply, i.e. that it results solely from open market operations by the central bank (case (i) on p. 37 above).

The substitution effects lower the market rates of return on financial assets (interest rates for brevity). Given transactions costs, this reduces the amount of these assets that it is worthwhile to hold in the intervals between receipts and payments, and increases the demand for money. Given individuals' expectations about future interest rates, the fall in current rates increases the number of individuals who are bearish about future asset prices. This also increases the demand for money.

But as time goes on, the experience of lower interest rates changes individuals' expectations in this respect. They come to expect lower interest rates in the future, which means a reduction in the amount of bearishness. The initial increase in the demand for money, on this score, therefore falls as time passes. The other side of this is, of course, an increasing demand for financial assets which lowers further the market interest rates on them. In particular the initial fall in short-term interest rates is now followed by reductions in longer-term interest rates and in the rates of return on shares.

Given the expected rates of return on real assets, the relative fall in interest rates makes it worthwhile for both firms and consumers to increase their current expenditures (investment) on durable goods; and this may be augmented by the wealth and expectations effects. The rise in current expenditures increases the demand for money. This is a further link – in addition to the interest-rate mechanism described above (on p. 42) – between portfolio decisions and current expenditure decisions.

So far attention has been concentrated on changes in three sets of variables in the demand for money function, namely interest rates, expected interest rates and the level of current expenditure.

But all these are mutually interdependent. Current interest rates help to determine the expected rates, and they also help to determine the level of current expenditure. And the latter, through its effect on the demand for money, helps to determine current interest rates. The ways in which the quantity demanded of money will be increased therefore depends on how these variables interact – and on the time lags in their interaction.

Thus a reduction in current interest rates may have little effect initially both on expected interest rates and on investment expenditures by firms and consumers (i.e. initially the elasticity of interest-rate expectations and the interest-elasticity of investment may both be small). At the outset, therefore, the quantity demanded of money will be increased to equality with the new supply mainly as a result of the fall in current interest rates relative to transactions costs and to the little-changed expected interest rates. Only a minor part of the increased demand for money will be due to the small increase in current expenditures.

But the longer the period of time for which a reduction in interest rates has ruled, the greater will be the effect of this reduction on interest-rate expectations (i.e. the elasticity of interest-rate expectations – for a given fall in the current rate – will increase with time). Similarly, the longer the period of time over which interest rates have been lower, the greater will be the effect of this – with given profit and income expectations – on the level of investment (i.e. the interest-elasticity of investment – for a given fall in interest rates – will increase with time).

Hence the ways in which an increase in the money supply is absorbed, by an increase in the demand for it, will depend on the length of time considered. The longer the time period allowed for, the greater will be that part of the increased demand for money which is due to a rise in current expenditures, and the smaller will be the part due to the fall in market interest rates relative to transactions costs and expected interest rates. This statement can be turned round to read : the longer the time period allowed, the greater will be the effect on current expenditures of an increase in the supply of money. But of course, as has been indicated, this conclusion depends on the assumption of given profit and income expectations – which will be considered in the next section.

The 'transmission mechanism', through which a change in the supply of money affects the aggregate demand for goods, is obviously a complicated one; and many economists will readily admit that it is not well understood. It has certainly been at the centre of the acute monetary controversy in recent years [17]. But it is now realised that the role of time lags in the mechanism requires much more study [32, 2] – as should have been evident from earlier writings of the best theorists in the field ([20] chap. 11).

The standard macro-economic model of the textbooks is usually referred to as 'Keynesian'. It is a comparative statics model in which expectations are taken as given without explanation, and in which the interest-elasticity of investment is often assumed to be small. As the analysis above has shown, these assumptions lead to the conclusion that an increase in the money supply will be absorbed to a significant extent by an increase in the demand for it due to a fall in market interest rates relative to expected interest rates. This reduces the effect of the change in the money supply on the level of aggregate demand, and provides the basis for Friedman's charge that 'money does not matter' in such models [11]. (The charge is, of course, only completely true if the economy is in the 'liquidity trap', where an increase in the money supply cannot lower the level of interest rates because *nobody* expects that they will fall. This is not the general case assumed by these models.)

In a recent book [29], Leijonhufvud has shown, *inter alia*, that these so-called 'Keynesian' models contain a poor represent-ation of the monetary theory of Keynes, as can be seen from his two major works. For Keynes it is long-term, rather than short-term, interest rates which are most important for the level of investment; and, in the monetary field, it is the Keynes wealth-effect that is important for the level of consumption. A change in the supply of money usually has its impact effect only on short-term rates. The effects of changes in them on long-term rates are constrained by individuals' expectations about future rates (see pp. 39–40 above) which may adjust only slowly through time. Keynes' conception of the interest-rate mechanism, connecting the supply of money and the aggregate demand for goods, was not that it was necessarily a weak mechanism – but rather that it could be slow in its operation if the central bank did not manipulate it in a decisive fashion. This comes out very clearly in the *Treatise* ([26] chap. 37); and in the *General Theory* ([27] chap. 15), variations in the speculative demand for money are the means used to explain how people's notion of 'a normal level' for interest rates constrains the movement of market interest rates ([29] chap. 5).

For Friedman [13], as for Keynes ([27] chap. 11), it is the interest-rate mechanism that explains the connection between the supply of money and the aggregate demand for goods. But Friedman, in contrast to Keynes, does not stress the role of interest-rate expectations in the determination of current interest rates. This is maybe surprising, since Friedman does stress the importance of expectations in another respect, namely the role of expectations about the future prices of goods in the demand for money function [9]. Nevertheless, he emphasises that the portfolio adjustments, following upon an increase in the supply of money, will take time to complete. There will be 'long and variable lags' in the relation between the supply of money and the aggregate demand for goods [10].

To that relation, however, must be added something more before the analysis of the restoration of monetary equilibrium can be completed. It is necessary to ask how the rise in aggregate demand, resulting from an increase in the money supply, will affect the levels of national output and prices, and what will be the effects of the latter changes on portfolio decisions.

6 Effects on Output and Prices

The connection between the supply of money and the levels of national output and prices depends on *all* the functional relations in the macro-economic working of a price system [35, 46]. But one problem is central to the construction of macro-economic models – and obviously so since the object of study is the price system. That problem is the way (or ways) in which the prices, of both goods and factors, adjust in conditions of disequilibrium.

There are two aspects to this matter. First, how is knowledge of disequilibrium acquired, i.e. how do buyers and/or sellers discover that quantities demanded and supplied are not equal at ruling prices? Second, how do buyers and/or sellers react to the fact that they are not buying or selling the quantities which they want to at existing prices? Answers to these questions are needed for the analysis of the effects of the supply of money on economic activity.

The form of modern macro-economic models is derived from Keynes' *General Theory*. But many textbook models are based on the assumptions that money wages and prices are inflexible in a downwards direction, and that they are flexible upwards only in conditions of excess aggregate demand at full employment (i.e. in conditions of 'demand inflation'). This sometimes gives the erroneous impression that Keynes always worked on the same assumptions; and it even leads to the absurd idea that his explanation of unemployment comes to no more than a downward inflexibility of money wages. In fact, Keynes analysed at considerable length the question of whether or not unemployment would be eliminated by a downward flexibility of money and prices ([27] chap. 19).

There are two major considerations in his analysis. First, if money wages and prices fall in conditions of unemployment, this will decrease the demand for money, which will lower interest rates (given the supply of money) and increase the volume of investment (thus a fall in money wages has the same effect as an increase in the supply of money). But the fall in interest rates will be constrained by inelastic interest-rate expectations (see above), and at most they can fall only to a zero level since there is the alternative of holding money at a zero interest return. Now it may be that the fall in interest rates will not be sufficient to raise investment to equality with the full-employment level of saving. If this were so, aggregate demand would be insufficient to promote full employment and a flexible price system would break down (since prices would continue to fall as long as there is un-employment).

Second, Keynes argued that a fall in prices, in conditions of unemployment, would engender expectations of a continuing de-flation. This would decrease the current volumes of investment and consumption and thus exacerbate the deflation. Hence a flexible price system would be liable to instability.

Moreover, Keynes developed this argument in a more general form which is of great importance for monetary theory ([27] chap. 17). Since money is necessarily an asset, it will be held and used only if people expect it to have a 'fairly' stable value. The value of money moves inversely with the price level. Hence, an essential pre-condition for the use of money is a 'fair' amount of stability in the price level. But this condition will not be fulfilled if the desired volume of investment is subject to considerable varia-tion. In those circumstances, a flexible price level would fluctuate to a considerable extent. Keynes maintained that the desired volume of investment is affected by many disturbances through time. He therefore concluded that a completely flexible price sys-tem is incompatible with the continued use of money [30]. This is his basic criticism of the 'classical' contention that a flexible-price, monetary economy would automatically ensure the full employment of resources.

Keynes' criticism stimulated the formulation of the 'Pigou-effect' as a means of defending the classical position. This is a wealth effect (not to be confused with the Keynes-effect) which arises from a change in the price level for *goods*. Thus if the prices of goods fall, as a result of unemployment, this increases the values of both money and financial assets in terms of goods. The real wealth of creditors is increased, and they will probably raise their (real) levels of consumption. But since the reverse will be true for debtors, the positive and negative wealth effects may be expected to cancel out, thus leaving aggregate (real) consumption unaffected. However, there may be *asymmetric* effects in the case of government debt. It may be that the holders of it are better off and will increase their (real) expenditures on consumption; and that the government is worse off but will not lower its (real) expenditures on that account.

On balance, therefore, this Pigou-effect of a fall in the price level may increase aggregate (real) expenditure and move the economy to the full-employment level. This counters Keynes' first criticism, given above, of the 'classical' mechanism for maintaining full employment, namely that the interest-rate mechanism, which is brought into operation by a fall in prices, may not be adequate to this end. But it does nothing to counter his second criticism – i.e. the incompatibility of a fluctuating price level and the continued use of money – since the Pigou-effect operates through a change in the price level.

The formulation of the Pigou-effect (together with the development of general equilibrium analysis) was responsible for the growth, in the two decades following the war, of a large body of literature devoted to the analysis of the flexible-price, monetary economy. This was dominated by Patinkin's work, and particularly by his book [37] which has added both to the content of modern monetary theory and to the understanding of the historical development of that theory. That work, however, seems to have had two major consequences for the current development of monetary theory.

The first was, ironically, to undermine any importance that had been given to the Pigou-effect. This was in part the result of further analysis of the possible asymmetric effects on creditors and debtors of a change in the price level. The community, as holders of interest-bearing government debt, is better off when the price level falls; but the same community, in its role as taxpayers, is worse off because of the prospective increase in the real burden of servicing and/or repaying government debt. The latter consideration, if it is taken into account by individuals, cancels out the former, thus leaving no net wealth effect when a fall in the price level increases the real value of interest-bearing government debt. Moreover, there will be no net wealth effect from the increase in the real value of demand deposits, since these are the liabilities of the commercial banks which are as much part of the economy as their customers for whom the deposits are assets (i.e. demand deposits are 'inside money' in the terminology of Gurley and Shaw ([18] chap. 3)). This leaves only cash (coin, central bank notes and deposits, i.e. 'outside money') through which the Pigou-effect can operate. It is in this emasculated form that the Pigou-effect becomes the 'real-balance effect' of Patinkin's analysis ([37] chap. 12). (The concepts of inside and outside money have entered into recent analyses of the welfare effects of the use of money [24].)

The second major consequence of the latter's work was to stimulate a new interest – in the context of monetary theory – in the question of the ways in which prices adjust in conditions of disequilibrium. As indicated above, this question has to be answered before it is possible to say what will be the effects on economic activity of a change in the supply of money. The answers given by a flexible-price model of the economy, like that of Patinkin, are very different from those which follow from the analytical framework within which Keynes worked. The contrast has been analysed by Clower [4].

Consider an economy in which the price of each good (and factor) is determined by an auction. The auctioneer in each market calls out different prices for the good in question (say in an ascending order) and notes the quantities demanded and supplied at each price. From the knowledge acquired in this way, he fixes the market price at the (equilibrium) level which equates the quantities demanded and supplied, and then allows production and trade to take place. With this arrangement, trading occurs only at equilibrium prices and never at disequilibrium ones. However, since all prices are mutually interdependent, the price in any one market has to be settled in relation to the prices in all other markets. It would be necessary, therefore, to have a 'supreme auctioneer' for the whole economy who would co-ordinate the decisions of all the lesser auctioneers in the different markets for goods and factors. It would be his job to find that *set* of all prices which would simultaneously equate demand and supply in every market (i.e. to find the mathematical solution to a Walrasian system of general equilibrium).

In such a system, adjustments in prices are taken care of by the auctioning process, and individual buyers and sellers are never called upon to react to disequilibrium situations. In particular, full employment of resources is necessarily maintained since prices are always fixed so as to equate the quantities demanded and supplied of factors. Most of Patinkin's monetary analysis is undertaken within a system of price determination like that just described; and it is maybe not surprising that he has some difficulty in expressing a theory of unemployment within it ([37] chap. 13; [5]).

Now consider an economy in which all goods are produced *in anticipation* of demand. Each firm puts its products on the market at the price which it *expects* to get for the quantity it supplies. But the price may not be an equilibrium one, because the quantity demanded at it is not equal to that supplied. The knowledge of this disequilibrium will come to the firm either in the form of an involuntary addition to inventories (when there is excess supply), or in the form of an involuntary rundown of inventories or lengthening of order books (when there is excess demand). That is, in contrast to the Patinkin model above, trading can take place at disequilibrium prices; there is not an auctioning process to prevent this. Hence the adjustment of disequilibrium prices will depend on how the buyers and/or sellers react to them.

A firm may react to a disequilibrium situation by changing either its price or the quantity it produces. If there is excess supply, it may lower price or cut output. But in an uncertain world it cannot be sure that the present price will be a disequilibrium one in the longer run. It may well therefore react, in the short run, by reducing output rather than price. That is, the speed of response of output, to disequilibrium, may be greater than that of price ([29] chap. 2).

It is this speed of response of prices (which is, of course, a question of time lags) which gives precision to the concept of 'price flexibility'. A perfectly flexible price system would be one in which *all* prices are adjusted immediately to equilibrium levels whenever the economy is disturbed; the auction-type system described above has this property. Less than perfect flexibility of prices is a matter of degree, which depends on the lengths of the time lags in the adjustment of prices. The longer are those lags, the greater will be the changes in outputs (or inventories) induced by a disturbance of the economy.

Although Keynes did not put the matter precisely in these terms, it now seems clear that he worked within an analytical framework of this character ([29] chap. 5). It certainly fits his separation of (i) the analysis of changes in output and employment through the multiplier ([27] chap. 10) from (ii) the analysis of the effects on national output of changes in the price level ([27] chap. 19). In the short run, excess aggregate supply will reduce output, employment and real income rather than the price level. The lower level of income will now constrain the demands for goods below what they would be at full employment. That is, in so far as *all* prices cannot be adjusted immediately to their equilibrium levels, the price system will not communicate full information to firms about the demands for goods that would be forthcoming from the supplies of factors which resource-owners wish to provide. In the longer run, when the price level does fall, it is not certain in what way this will affect the level of national output (see p. 51 above).

TIME LAGS

Changes in prices (including wage rates) are in fact subject to time lags. But the analytical study of how these operate has only recently attracted much attention [38]. This means, unfortunately, that we do not yet have an adequate macroeconomic model into which to fit the monetary analysis of Section 5 above. One can only sketch some possibilities.

An increase in the supply of money will cause a time-lagged reduction in interest rates. *Given* the expected rates of return on real assets (expected profits for brevity), this will raise current expenditures on goods. But expected profits may be changing during the time taken for interest rates to fall. The level of expected profits at any moment depends on expected outputs and prices, and these expectations will be influenced by recent changes in outputs and prices. The more rapidly an economy has been expanding, the more optimistic will its firms be about prospective profits. But if the growth rate declines, or if the economy moves into a recession, this will gradually dampen profit expectations. The rate *over time* at which expected profits change therefore depends on two things. It depends partly on the time lags in the formation of profit expectations on the basis of past profit experience, and partly on the time lags in the changes in the prices and outputs which determine actual profits.

It is the time-rate of change in interest rates *relative* to the time-rate of change in expected profits that determines the magnitude of the effect on current expenditures of a given increase in the supply of money. Suppose that expected profits are falling because of a slow-down in the growth of output, and that the supply of money is now increased. Interest rates begin to fall, but expected profits also continue to do the same. The more rapidly interest rates are brought down relatively to the falling expected profits, the greater will be the effect of the increase in the supply of money upon current expenditures.

But, as was seen in Section 5 above, there is a two-way interaction between portfolio decisions and current expenditures. On the one hand, the supply of money – through its effect on the relation between interest rates and expected profits – helps to determine current expenditures, which in their turn – through their effect on realised profits – help to determine expected profits. On the other hand, expected profits – through their effect on current expenditures – help to determine the demand for money, which in its turn – through its relation to the supply of money – helps to determine interest rates. Moreover, there are time lags operating in both of these chains of cause and effect between portfolio decisions and current expenditures. It is not possible therefore, without a precise knowledge of the structure of these time lags, and of how they interact, to predict the effects on interest rates and current expenditures of a given increase in the supply of money.

One possible outcome, for example, of the latter change is

that interest rates may fluctuate [28, 48]. Initially they will fall in order to induce the absorption into portfolios of the increased money supply, while current expenditures remain more or less unchanged. But as the latter rise, in response to lower interest rates, this will increase the demand for money which will tend to pull interest rates up again (though the extent of this will depend on what has been happening to interest-rate expectations in the meantime). Moreover, the rise in current expenditures, by raising national output and/or the price level, will gradually improve profit expectations, and this will increase current expenditures still further. Hence the continuing increase in the demand for money may pull interest rates above their initial level. But that will depend upon what happens to profit expectations in the chain of events following upon the increase in the supply of money.

The analysis above may suggest that the connection between the supply of money and the levels of national output and prices is a *complex* one–i.e. that it is not one which is subject to a few generalisations that will cover all situations. This was certainly Keynes' view ([27] chap. 21).

But to say that the connection is complex, is not to say that it is necessarily *tenuous*. It would indeed be very surprising to find that a man, who gave so much time to monetary theory, thought that 'money does not matter'. Nevertheless there are economists, expressing themselves within a 'Keynesian' framework, who do suggest a somewhat tenuous connection between the supply of money and the levels of national output and prices ([39] chap. 6; [40]).

Their argument is basically that the demand for money (or its inverse, the desired velocity of circulation of money) is 'very' variable. But that needs explanation. It implies that the quantity demanded of money adjusts to the quantity supplied without having much effect on the level of expenditure on goods. This would be so if (i) the demand for money is highly responsive to a change in interest rates, and/or (ii) investment is little responsive to a change in interest rates. Both these propositions have been analysed at earlier stages. The truth or falsehood of (i) in any situation depends on what is happening to interest-rate expectations (see pp. 39–40 above). The truth or falsehood of

(ii) in any situation depends on what is happening to profit expectations (see pp. 55–6 above).

Friedman frequently contrasts his own position with that of Keynes and the 'Keynesians' (who, however, as has been seen, must be distinguished from each other). A comparative study of the writings on money of Keynes and Friedman can be a fascinating matter, particularly for those who are under the impression that there is little similarity in their views. In so far as the contrast between them can be summed up in a simple form, it is that Friedman sees a more *systematic* connection between the supply of money and the levels of national output and prices than does Keynes. The explanation for this once again involves propositions (i) and (ii) of the previous paragraph. Friedman appears to think that interest-rate expectations adapt fairly quickly to recent experience, so that the whole range of market interest rates will respond fairly quickly to a change in the supply of money; and that profit (and income) expectations do not adapt quickly to recent experience, so that they are fairly stable in the short run [11, 12]. Keynes was concerned that the reverse situations in both respects might occur together ([27] chap. 22). It is, of course, striking that both writers are making (different) *asymmetric* assumptions about the formation of the two sets of expectations.

If Friedman's assumptions are correct for all situations, there will be a systematic connection between the supply of money and the levels of national output and prices, even after 'long and variable lags'. If Keynes' scepticism is justified, the connection will be more complex. The dispute is essentially one of whether or not the connection between money and economic activity can be stated in a few generalisations.

How systematic, or how complex, is the connection can, however, be decided only by reference to the facts – as Friedman frequently emphasises, and demonstrates by his own empirical research [14]. But as his and other econometric studies have shown so far, it is exceedingly difficult to disentangle, within the available data, the lines of cause and effect through which money and economic activity have interacted [49]. Nor is it possible to do that disentagling without hypotheses as too how the facts may be interrelated. That is why one must start with monetary theory.

Select Bibliography

ABBREVIATIONS

A.E.R.	*American Economic Review*
E.J.	*Economic Journal*
J.M.C.B.	*Journal of Money, Credit and Banking*
J.P.E.	*Journal of Political Economy*
O.E.P.	*Oxford Economic Papers (New Series)*
Q.J.E.	*Quarterly Journal of Economics*
R.E.Stats.	*Review of Economics and Statistics*
W.E.J.	*Western Economic Journal*

[1] W. J. Baumol, 'The Transactions Demand for Cash: An Inventory Theory Approach', *Q.J.E.*, LXVI (1952).

[2] W. C. Brainard and J. Tobin, 'Pitfalls in Financial Model Building, *A.E.R.*, LVIII (1968).

[3] P. Cagan, *Determinants and Effects of Changes in the Stock of Money, 1875–1960* (Columbia U.P. for N.B.E.R., New York, 1965).

[4] R. W. Clower, 'The Keynesian Counterrevolution: A Theoretical Appraisal', in F. H. Hahn and F. P. R. Brechling (eds.), *The Theory of Interest Rates* (Macmillan, London, 1965).

[5] R. W. Clower, 'A Reconsideration of the Microfoundations of Monetary Theory', *W.E.J.*, VI (1967), reprinted in [6] below.

[6] R. W. Clower, Introduction to R. W. Clower (ed.), *Monetary Theory, Selected Readings* (Penguin Books, Harmondsworth, 1969).

[7] A. B. Cramp, 'Financial Theory and Control of Bank Deposits', *O.E.P.*, xx (1968).

[8] M. Fleming, 'The Timing of Payments and the Demand for Money', *Economica*, xxxi (1964).

[9] M. Friedman, 'The Quantity Theory of Money – A Restatement', in M. Friedman (ed.), *Studies in the Quantity Theory of Money* (Chicago U.P., 1956), reprinted in M. Freidman, *The Optimum Quantity of Money* Chicago U.P., 1969).

[10] M. Friedman, 'The Lag in Effect of Monetary Policy', *J.P.E.*, lxix (1961), reprinted in M. Friedman, *The Optimum Quantity of Money* (Chicago U.P., 1969).

[11] M. Friedman, 'The Monetary Theory and Policy of Henry Simons', *Journal of Law and Economics*, x (1967), reprinted in M. Friedman, *The Optimum Quantity of Money* (Chicago U.P., 1969).

[12] M. Friedman, 'A Theoretical Framework for Monetary Analysis', *J.P.E.*, lxxviii (1970).

[13] M. Friedman and A. J. Schwartz, 'Money and Business Cycles', *R.E.Stats.*, xlv (1963), reprinted in M. Friedman, *The Optimum Quantity of Money* (Chicago U.P., 1969).

[14] M. Friedman and A. J. Schwartz, *A Monetary History of the United States, 1867–1960* (Princeton U.P., 1963).

[15] M. Friedman and A. J. Schwartz, *Monetary Statistics of the United States* (Columbia U.P. for N.B.E.R., New York, 1970).

[16] J. A. Galbraith, 'Monetary Policy and Nonbank Financial Intermediaries', *National Banking Review*, iv (1966), reprinted in J. Lindauer (ed.), *Macroeconomic Readings*, (Collier–Macmillan, New York, 1968).

[17] C. A. E. Goodhart and A. D. Crockett, 'The Importance of Money', *Bank of England Quarterly Bulletin*, x (1970).

[18] J. G. Gurley and E. S. Shaw, *Money in a Theory of Finance* (Brookings Institution, Washington, 1960).

[19] J. R. Hicks, 'A Suggestion for Simplifying the Theory of Money', *Economica*, ii (1935), reprinted in [21] below.

[20] J. R. Hicks, *A Contribution to the Theory of the Trade Cycle* (Oxford U.P., 1950).

[21] J. R. Hicks, *Critical Essays in Monetary Theory* (Oxford U.P., 1967).

[22] D. M. Jaffee and F. Modigliani, 'A Theory and Test of Credit Rationing', *A.E.R.*, LIX (1969).

[23] H. G. Johnson, 'Monetary Theory and Policy', *A.E.R.*, LII (1962), reprinted in H. G. Johnson, *Essays in Monetary Economics* (Allen & Unwin, London, 1967).

[24] H. G. Johnson, 'Inside Money, Outside Money, Income, Wealth, and Welfare in Monetary Theory', *J.M.C.B.*, I (1969).

[25] H. G. Johnson, 'Recent Developments in Monetary Theory: A Commentary', in D. R. Croome and H. G. Johnson (ed.), *Money in Britain, 1959–69* (Oxford U.P., 1970).

[26] J. M. Keynes, *A Treatise on Money*, 2 vols. (Macmillan, London, 1930).

[27] J. M. Keynes, *The General Theory of Employment, Interest and Money* (Macmillan, London, 1936).

[28] D. Laidler, 'The Permanent-Income Concept in a Macro-Economic Model', *O.E.P.*, XX (1968).

[29] A Leijonhufvud, *On Keynesian Economics and the Economics of Keynes* (Oxford U.P., 1968).

[30] A. P. Lerner, 'The Essential Properties of Interest and Money', *Q.J.E.*, LXVI (1952), reprinted in A. P. Lerner, *Essays in Economic Analysis* (Macmillan, London, 1953).

[31] B. G. Malkiel, *The Term Structure of Interest Rates* (Princeton U.P., 1966).

[32] T. Mayer, 'The Lag Effect in Monetary Policy: Some Criticisms', *W.E.J.*, V (1967).

[33] D. Meiselman, *The Term Structure of Interest Rates* (Prentice–Hall, Englewood Cliffs, N.J., 1962).

[34] H. L. Miller, Jr., 'On "Liquidity" and "Transactions Costs"', *Southern Economic Journal*, XXXII (1965).

[35] F. Modigliani, 'The Monetary Mechanism and its Interaction with Real Phenomena', *R.E.Stats*, XLV (1963).

[36] E. V. Morgan, 'The Essential Qualities of Money', *Manchester School*, XXXVII (1969).

[37] D. Patinkin, *Money, Interest and Prices*, 2nd ed. (Harper & Row, New York, 1965).

[38] E. S. Phelps *et al.*, *Microeconomic Foundations of Employment and Inflation Theory* (Norton, New York, 1970).

[39] (Radcliffe) Committee on the Working of the Monetary System, *Report*, Cmnd. 827 (H.M.S.O., London, 1959).

[40] R. S. Sayers, 'Monetary Thought and Monetary Policy in England', *E.J.*, LXX (1960).

[41] W. L. Smith, 'Financial Intermediaries and Monetary Controls', *Q.J.E.*, LXXIII (1959).

[42] J. Tobin, 'The Interest-Elasticity of Transactions Demand for Cash', *R.E.Stats.*, XXXVIII (1956).

[43] J. Tobin, 'Liquidity Preference as Behaviour Towards Risk', *Review of Economic Studies*, XXV (1958), reprinted in D. D. Hester and J. Tobin (ed.), *Risk Aversion and Portfolio Choice*, Cowles Foundation Monograph 19 (Wiley, New York, 1967).

[44] J. Tobin, 'Commercial Banks as Creators of "Money" ', in D. Carson (ed.), *Banking and Monetary Studies* (Irwin, Homewood, Ill., 1963), reprinted in D. D. Hester and J. Tobin (eds.), *Financial Markets and Economic Activity*, Cowles Foundation Monograph 21 (Wiley, New York, 1967).

[45] J. Tobin, 'The Theory of Portfolio Selection', in F. H. Hahn and F. P. R. Brechling (eds.), *The Theory of Interest Rates* (Macmillan, London, 1965).

[46] J. Tobin, 'A General Equilibrium Approach to Monetary Theory', *J.M.C.B.*, I (1969).

[47] J. Tobin and R. C. Brainard, 'Financial Intermediaries and the Effectiveness of Monetary Controls', *A.E.R.*, LIII (1963), reprinted in D. D. Hester and J. Tobin (eds.), *Financial Markets and Economic Activity*, Cowles Foundation Monograph 21 (Wiley, New York, 1967).

[48] D. Tucker, 'Dynamic Income Adjustments to Money Supply Changes', *A.E.R.*, LVI (1966).

[49] A. A. Walters, 'The Radcliffe Report – Ten Years After : A Survey of Empirical Evidence', in D. R. Croome and H. G. Johnson (eds.), *Money in Britain, 1959–69* (Oxford U.P., 1970).

[50] L. B. Yeager, 'Essential Properties of the Medium of Exchange', *Kyklos*, XXI (1968), reprinted in R. W. Clower (ed.), *Monetary Theory, Selected Readings* (Penguin Books, Harmondsworth, 1969).